OCTOPUSES

by Jenny Markert

Published in the United States of America by The Child's World®
1980 Lookout Drive • Mankato, MN 56003-1705
800-599-READ • www.childsworld.com

PHOTO CREDITS
All photos © Brandon Cole/www.brandoncole.com except:
© A & C Mahaney/SeaPics.com: 10–11
© Anthony Mercieca/Photo Researchers, Inc.: 9
© David Fleetham/Getty Images: 28–29
© iStockphoto.com/Frank Sebastian Hansen: 2, 30
© Marc Chamberlain/SeaPics.com: 25

ACKNOWLEDGMENTS
The Child's World®: Mary Berendes, Publishing Director;
Katherine Stevenson, Editor; Pamela Mitsakos, Photo Researcher;
Judy Karren, Fact Checker

The Design Lab: Kathleen Petelinsek, Design and Page Production

LIBRARY OF CONGRESS CATALOGING-IN-PUBLICATION DATA
Markert, Jenny.
  Octopuses / by Jenny Markert.
    p. cm. — (New naturebooks)
  Includes index.
  ISBN-13: 978-1-59296-849-7 (library bound : alk. paper)
  ISBN-10: 1-59296-849-X (library bound : alk. paper)
  1. Octopuses—Juvenile literature. I. Title.
  QL430.3.O2M37 2007
  594'.56—dc22   2006103444

Table of Contents

On the cover: Here you can see a day octopus as it swims off the coast of Hawai‘i. Day octopuses get their name because they prefer to hunt for food during the daytime.

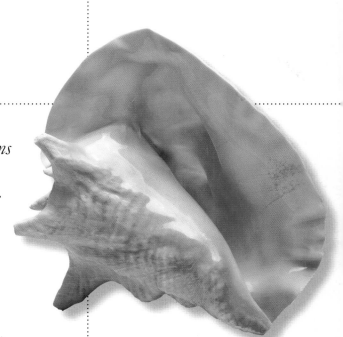

Meet the Octopus!

The word "octopus" comes from the Greek language. It means "eight-footed one."

Octopuses have been given scary names, such as "devil fish," because of their appearance.

If an octopus loses an arm, it can grow a new one.

A crab sits on the ocean bottom, far beneath the waves. Fish swim back and forth, paying no attention. Then a strange, eight-armed creature glides smoothly across the rocks. The creature comes closer. Its arms wrap around the crab— and the clam disappears, to become dinner. Only pieces of shell remain. The eight-armed creature glides away again. What is this underwater hunter? It's an octopus!

Common octopuses like this one hunt at night. This one is hunting along the ocean floor in the Caribbean Sea. Common octopuses grow to be about 3 feet (1 m) long.

What Do Octopuses Look Like?

Octopuses are cephalopods (SEH-fuh-luh-podz). Squids and cuttlefish are cephalopods, too. Other cephalopods have shells on the outsides or the insides of their bodies, but octopuses don't.

People use suction cups, too—such as the rubbery cups on bathmats that stick to the bottom of the tub.

Octopuses have very different bodies from yours. They don't have a bony skeleton. They don't have a shell, either, as many underwater animals too. They have soft, baglike bodies instead. Without bones or shells, they can move quickly and freely. They can squeeze themselves into tiny openings.

The octopus's eight arms are its most striking feature. The arms are attached to the animal's head, not its body. Long and muscular, they can coil and twist in any direction. Under each arm are rows of **suction cups**. The octopus uses them for grasping rocks and slippery food and for tasting things. Octopuses use certain arms for certain things. They use their front arms more for gathering food. They use their back arms more for walking.

Red octopuses like this one live in the Pacific Ocean. These small octopuses grow only about as big as an adult person's hand.

6

Are There Different Kinds of Octopuses?

Some octopuses that live in deeper areas have winglike fins. Living so far underwater makes these octopuses hard to study. Scientists have much to learn about them.

There are over 200 different kinds, or **species**, of octopuses. Nobody knows the exact number. Many kinds haven't even been named or described yet. Octopuses live throughout the world's oceans, from warm coral reefs to the icy seas of Antarctica. Most of them live in shallow water. But some live in much deeper parts of the ocean.

Octopuses vary in their colors and patterns. They vary in size, too. The smallest is the Californian octopus. It is only about an inch (between 2 and 3 cm) long. Another kind called the common octopus is about the size of a skateboard. The giant Pacific octopus can grow to 30 feet (9 m) long. That's as long as a school bus! It can weigh 100 pounds (45 kg) or even more.

This tiny Californian octopus is resting on a piece of seaweed. The photographer almost swam right by it!

8

Are Octopuses Dangerous?

Blue-ringed octopuses live around Australia and the South Pacific. They're only about the size of golf balls. They don't attack people on purpose. But people have been bitten when they bother the animals or step on them.

Octopuses might look scary, but they are mainly shy, harmless animals. They would much rather hide than attack a person. But like other animals, octopuses can be dangerous when they are bothered or frightened.

Blue-ringed octopuses, however, are very dangerous. Usually these small animals are a brownish color with dull blue rings. If they get angry or excited, they turn yellow with bright blue spots. Their bite carries poisonous **venom** into their victim. The venom stops the victim's muscles from moving—including the muscles for breathing. A small amount of venom from a blue-ringed octopus can kill a person in only minutes!

Do you think this blue-ringed octopus is calm or upset?

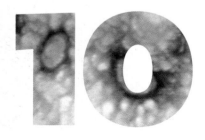

10

Are Octopuses Smart?

An octopus can figure out how to unscrew a jar lid to get at the food inside.

Octopuses sometimes use stones as "tools" to help build their dens or pry open clamshells.

Zoos and aquariums that keep octopuses often give them toys and games. That helps keep the animals from getting bored.

Octopuses are very smart! In fact, some people say that they are as smart as housecats. Sometimes an octopus runs into a problem, such as getting food from a hard-to-reach area. It will try many different ways of solving the problem. Once it succeeds, it remembers the answer for next time.

When people keep octopuses inside, they put them in a tank or aquarium. Octopuses are very good at getting out of these tanks! They have been known to crawl to another aquarium to eat the animals inside. In the wild, they sometimes break into crab or lobster traps to steal animals caught inside.

This veined octopus is using a conch shell (bottom) and a coconut to make a shelter. In fact, these octopuses use coconut shells so often, they are also called "coconut octopuses."

Where Do Octopuses Live?

Octopuses often use shells or rocks to block the entrances to their dens.

Octopuses have excellent senses of sight, smell, and touch.

An octopus has three hearts—and blue blood!

Regardless of their size, octopuses are shy and secretive. They prefer to live alone. They make their dens in rocky caves, coral reefs, and shipwrecks. They crawl into cracks and gaps in rocks. Some of their dens are very hard to see. Small octopuses sometimes live in empty seashells. Some even live in human garbage, such as pop bottles or tin cans. Octopuses usually leave their dens only to avoid a nosy enemy or to find food.

This giant Pacific octopus has made its den between some rocks. It is peeking out to be sure the photographer isn't an enemy.

What Do Octopuses Eat?

An octopus's toothed tongue is called a *radula*.

An octupus's beak is the biggest hard part on its body— and it's still very small. That's why the animal can squeeze itself into such tiny spaces.

Octopuses are **predators** that eat other underwater animals. Their **prey** includes shelled creatures such as crabs, lobsters, scallops, and clams. They eat fish, too, and even other octopuses. Sometimes octopuses collect a pile of oysters or clams. They use their arms and suction cups to pull the shells apart and get to the meat inside. Sometimes they use their bodies to cover a likely-looking spot on the ocean bottom. They poke their arms and suction cups around and pull out animals to eat.

Breaking into shelled animals isn't easy. Octopuses have special mouthparts and produce special juices that help. The mouthparts drill through the shell, and the juices weaken it. The juices break down the prey's insides, too. The octopus uses its toothed tongue and hard, parrotlike beak to break up and scrape up the meat inside.

This Caribbean reef octopus is hunting at night. Like most octopuses, it "parachutes" over its prey. The prey can't escape, and the octopus can enjoy its meal.

How Do Octopuses Move?

Scientists have seen two types of octopus "walking" along the ocean floor on only two arms! The animals use two of their back arms like tank treads, rolling them along.

Octopuses usually use their arms to crawl along the ocean bottom. They feel around with their arms and suckers as they go. But to catch prey or escape, they can swim very quickly for short distances. The main part of an octopus's body is covered by a muscular *mantle*. When the octopus wants to move fast, its pulls water into its mantle, puffing it up like a water balloon. The mantle's muscles push the water out through a tube called a funnel or *siphon*. The rushing water shoots the octopus through the water like a jet!

This day octopus is swimming quickly away from the photographer. Its siphon is wide open as it pushes water outward.

18

What Are Baby Octopuses Like?

A male octopus lives for only a few months after mating. He stops eating, his body slows down, and he dies.

In her whole lifetime, a female octopus lays only a single batch of eggs.

Female blue-ringed octopuses don't lay their eggs in dens. They carry the eggs with them until they hatch.

Besides using their dens for hiding, female octopuses use them for having their young. After mating, a female lays her eggs. The number of eggs depends on the kind of octopus. Some kinds can lay over 100,000 eggs! The female strings the eggs along the walls of her den. After she lays them, she stays nearby, protecting and cleaning them. She doesn't eat while she is caring for the eggs.

When the eggs finally hatch, the tiny babies are on their own. Their mother dies soon afterward. The baby octopuses face many dangers. They are as small as fleas and cannot swim. They drift in the ocean, hoping to avoid hungry sea creatures. Only a few baby octopuses are lucky enough to survive their first year.

This giant Pacific octopus mother is guarding her eggs. The little black spots on each egg are the babies' eyes.

How Do Octopuses Stay Safe?

Scientists have discovered one deep-water octopus with unusual suckers. The suckers don't cling to things well, but they glow in the dark!

Even as adults, octopuses still face many dangers. Many predators such as large fish, seals, otters, and moray eels like to eat them. Luckily, octopuses are good at hiding and escaping. They choose their dens and hiding places well. Special coloring called **camouflage** helps them blend in with their surroundings. Octopuses are often white with red or gray dots. Next to coral or rocky sea bottoms, they are very hard to see.

Can you find the day octopus in this picture?

22

What mood do you think this octopus is in?

To blend in even better, an octopus can actually change colors! Waves of different colors can flow across its skin. The octopus can turn red, green, or even black. Its skin can change patterns, too. It can show stripes, solid colors, or dots. It might turn smooth or bumpy to match the surface underneath.

Scientists think that octopuses also change colors to show their moods. Frightened octopuses turn pale, light colors. Angry octopuses might be solid purple or black. When they eat, octopuses often have spotted, blotchy colors. The only parts of an octopus that don't change color are its white suckers and the gill slits it uses for breathing.

Tiny sacs under the octopus's skin hold coloring, or pigment. The octopus squeezes the sacs to show different amounts of color.

Mimic octopuses of the Pacific can make themselves look and move like fish or sea snakes.

The fish around this day octopus kept bothering it. The octopus turned darker as it became angrier and angrier.

25

Even if color changes don't confuse an enemy, many octopuses have another trick. Instead of staying to fight, they make a clever escape. Their bodies have sacs that produce a dark, inky liquid. When the enemy attacks, the octopus squirts this ink into the water. The cloud of ink looks like the octopus. It throws off the attacker's sense of smell, too. When the enemy attacks, it finds only an inky blob. Meanwhile, the octopus darts away to safety—often changing color to confuse the enemy even more.

Some octopuses drop one wriggling arm to confuse an attacker while they get away.

Most deep-sea octopuses don't have ink sacs. Deep underwater, there's too little light for inky clouds to help.

This octopus felt threatened by nearby divers. You can see the ink cloud it created as it tried to get away.

Are Octopuses in Danger?

People in many parts of the world eat octopus.

Octopuses don't live very long. Smaller kinds might live six months, while the biggest ones might live three to four years.

There aren't any laws protecting octopuses. In fact, people fish for them in many parts of the world. There is still a lot to learn about these creatures! No one even knows if any kinds are **endangered** or threatened. Like many sea creatures, they can be harmed by polluted water. Scientists will keep studying them to find out more.

Octopuses might live in hidden caves and sunken ships, but they aren't the monsters we imagine them to be. These shy, harmless animals have many clever ways of avoiding danger and catching food. In fact, they are some of the most amazing of all Earth's underwater creatures!

You can see all of this day octopus's arms as it swims near Kona, Hawai'i.

28

Glossary

camouflage (KA-muh-flazh) Camouflage is special coloring or markings that help an animal blend in with its surroundings. Octopuses have amazing camouflage.

endangered (in-DAYN-jurd) An endangered animal is one that is close to dying out completely. No one knows if any octopuses are endangered.

pigment (PIG-munt) Pigment is a substance that gives color to something, including a plant or animal. Octopuses squeeze sacs of pigment in their skin to change color.

predators (PREH-duh-terz) Predators are animals that hunt and kill other animals for food. Octopuses are predators.

prey (PRAY) Prey are animals that other animals hunt as food. Shellfish are common prey for octopuses.

species (SPEE-sheez) An animal species is a group of animals that share the same features and can have babies only with animals in the same group. There are over 200 species of octopus.

suction cups (SUK-shun KUPZ) Suction cups are soft cups that cling to a surface when they are flattened against it. Octopuses have suction cups on their arms.

venom (VEH-num) Venom is a poisonous substance some animals produce. They can harm other animals with it, usually by biting or stinging. The blue-ringed octopus produces a deadly venom.

To Find Out More

Read It!

Hunt, James C. *Octopus and Squid.* Monterey, CA: Monterey Bay Aquarium, 1996.

Kalman, Bobbie, Rebecca Sjonger, and Margaret Amy Reiach. *The Amazing Octopus.* New York: Crabtree Publishing, 2003.

Langeland, Deirdre, and Steven Petruccio (illustrator). *Octopus' Den.* Norwalk, CT: Soundprints, 1997.

Rhodes, Mary Jo, and David Hall (photographer). *Octopuses and Squids.* New York: Children's Press, 2005.

Wallace, Karen, and Mike Bostock (illustrator). *Gentle Giant Octopus.* Cambridge, MA: Candlewick Press, 2002.

On the Web

Visit our Web page for lots of links about octopuses:
http://www.childsworld.com/links

Note to Parents, Teachers, and Librarians: We routinely check our Web links to make sure they're safe, active sites—so encourage your readers to check them out!

31

Index